No Lex 11-12

EXPLORERS!

La Salle
Explorer of the Mississippi

Arlene Bourgeois Molzahn

Enslow Publishers, Inc.

40 Industrial Road   PO Box 38
Box 398   Aldershot
Berkeley Heights, NJ 07922   Hants GU12 6BP
USA   UK

http://www.enslow.com

To my grandson, Christopher Joseph,
who has brought so much joy to our family.

Library of Congress Cataloging-in-Publication Data

Molzahn, Arlene Bourgeois.
    La Salle : explorer of the Mississippi / Arlene Bourgeois Molzahn.
        p. cm. — (Explorers!)
    Summary: Discusses the life of Rene-Robert Cavelier, Sieur de La Salle and his explorations of the Ohio and
Mississippi Rivers.
    Includes bibliographical references and index.
    ISBN 0-7660-2141-6
    1. La Salle, Robert Cavelier, sieur de, 1643-1687—Juvenile literature. 2. Explorers—Mississippi River
Valley—Biography—Juvenile literature. 3. Explorers—France—Biography—Juvenile literature. 4. Mississippi
River Valley—Discovery and exploration—French—Juvenile literature. 5. Ohio River Valley—Discovery and
exploration—French—Juvenile literature. 6. Mississippi River Valley—History—To 1803—Juvenile literature.
7. Canada—History—To 1763 (New France)—Juvenile literature. [1. La Salle, Robert Cavelier, sieur de,
1643–1687. 2. Explorers. 3. Mississippi River—Discovery and exploration. 4. America—Discovery and
exploration—French.] I. Title. II. Explorers! (Enslow Publishers)
F352.M655 2004
977.'01'092—dc21   2003002264

Printed in the United States of America

10 9 8 7 6 5 4 3 2 1

To Our Readers: We have done our best to make sure all Internet Addresses in this book were active and appropriate
when we went to press. However, the author and the publisher have no control over and assume no liability for the
material available on those Internet sites or on other Web sites they may link to. Any comments or suggestions can be
sent by e-mail to comments@enslow.com or to the address on the back cover.

Every effort has been made to locate all copyright holders of material used in this book. If any errors or omissions
have occurred, corrections will be made in future editions of this book.

Illustration Credits: © 1996-2003 ArtToday.com, Inc., pp. 10 (top), 16 (landscapes), 22 (inset), 34
(portrait); © 1999 Artville, LLC., pp. 28; Corel Corporation, p. 15; Enslow Publishers, Inc., pp. 4, 16,
34 (map); Library of Congress, pp. 1, 10 (bottom), 12, 13, 14, 18, 19, 20, 21, 22 (background), 24, 25,
26 (all), 30, 31, 32, 36, 37, 38, 40, 42, 43, 44; Courtesy of the Texas Historical Commission, pp. 6, 7 (top
and bottom), 8 (top and bottom), 9.

Cover Illustration: background, Monster Zero Media; portrait, Enslow Publishers, Inc.

Please note: Compasses on the cover and in the book are from © 1999 Artville, LLC.

Contents

La Salle sailed from France to America to start a new settlement.

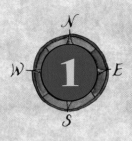

Belle

In 1684, La Salle set off from France with four ships. About 300 people sailed with him. They were going to start a settlement in America.

Just a few years before, La Salle had found the Mississippi River and the lands around it. He thought these lands would be good for farming and the fur trade. He talked to King Louis XIV of France. King Louis gave La Salle ships for his trip. La Salle and his ships sailed to America.

The trip was filled with adventure from the time they left. In September, one of the ships was captured by Spanish pirates. Then one ship ran aground. A third ship

In 1997, crews from the Texas Historical Commission worked to save what was left of *Belle*. Here is the hull of the ship.

sailed back to France. The fourth ship sailed safely into Matagorda Bay in what is now Texas. This ship was *Belle*. La Salle did not know he was about 400 miles west of the Mississippi River.

The remaining people built Fort St. Louis in what is today Victoria County, Texas. La Salle

Here a crane is lifting a cannon which was once on *Belle*, out of the water. The crew takes a close look at it.

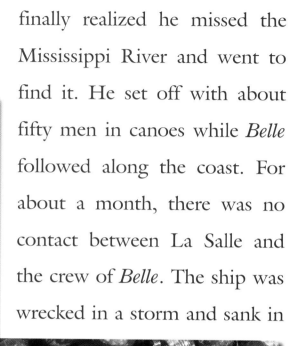

Among the several things found on *Belle* was this colander. Brass bells were also found.

finally realized he missed the Mississippi River and went to find it. He set off with about fifty men in canoes while *Belle* followed along the coast. For about a month, there was no contact between La Salle and the crew of *Belle*. The ship was wrecked in a storm and sank in

Matagorda Bay. In 1687, a Spanish expedition found the remains of *Belle*.

Over 300 years later, in 1997, crews from the Texas Historical Commission worked to save what was left of *Belle*. The hull was found buried in the sand. The hull is the outside shell of a ship. The crews found brass bells, a brass cannon, jars, and even a skeleton. This amazing discovery has helped us learn more about La Salle and his expedition.

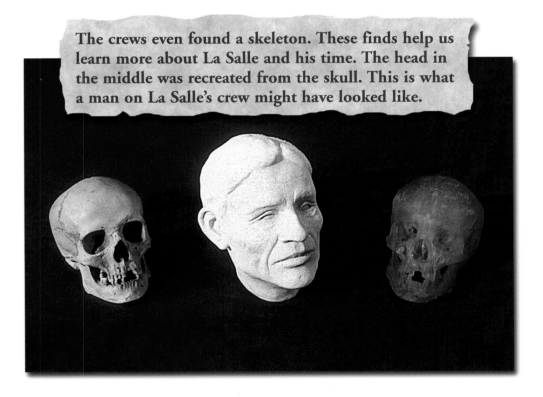

The crews even found a skeleton. These finds help us learn more about La Salle and his time. The head in the middle was recreated from the skull. This is what a man on La Salle's crew might have looked like.

La Salle was born in Rouen, France, as René-Robert Cavelier. The old map below shows Rouen at that time. To the left is the cathedral in Rouen.

Sieur de La Salle

La Salle was born on November 22, 1643, in Rouen, France, as René-Robert Cavelier. His mother was Catherine Geeset and his father was Jean Cavelier. He had two brothers and a sister. One brother was a priest who went to live in Montreal, Canada. The other brother was a lawyer who died when La Salle was quite young.

The family made a lot of money from the trading business that they owned. They also owned a huge estate called La Salle. René-Robert Cavelier took the name Sieur de La Salle, which is French for "the gentleman from La Salle." His full name became René-Robert Cavelier, Sieur de La Salle.

La Salle studied nine years to become a priest. He was a good student, but he wanted a life of adventure. So he decided not to become a priest.

In the summer of 1667, La Salle sailed to Montreal in New France in Canada. His brother lived there with several priests. These priests owned land west of Montreal along the St. Lawrence River. The priests

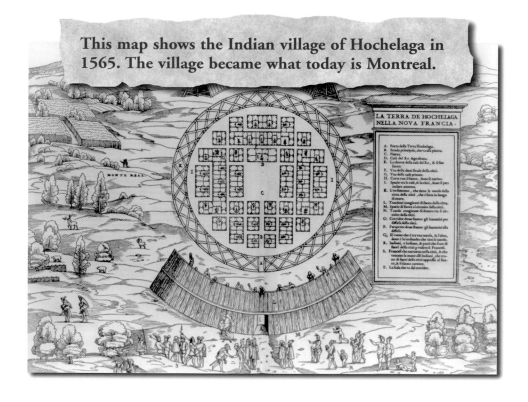

This map shows the Indian village of Hochelaga in 1565. The village became what today is Montreal.

The Fur Trade

The fur trade played a big part in the development of Canada and the United States. It began in the 1500s between American Indians and Europeans. The American Indians traded furs for items like tools and weapons. The Europeans used the fur to make hats and other clothing items. The demand for fur led people to settle and explore North America. Fur traders and trappers built trading posts in the wilderness. Some of these settlements became big cities, such as New Orleans and St. Louis in the United States, and Montreal and Quebec in Canada.

The fur trade was very important to the American Indians and the Europeans.

agreed to give La Salle a large amount of the land they owned. In return, La Salle promised to try to get other people from France to come to Canada and America.

La Salle wrote letters to people in France telling them about the good land in Canada and America. Many settlers from France came to settle in or near Montreal. La Salle cleared a large part of his land and began

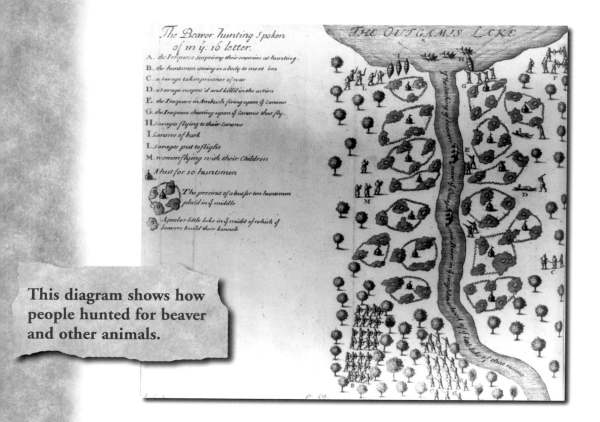

This diagram shows how people hunted for beaver and other animals.

Beaver fur was important to the fur trade.

farming. He also traded for furs with the Indians. After only two years of farming and fur trading, La Salle became rich. But he was not happy. He did not want to be a farmer or a fur trader. He wanted to discover and explore new lands.

La Salle was told about the "big water"—the Mississippi River. La Salle wanted to explore this river. He hoped it would lead to an all-water route through North America.

New France

Great Lakes

MISSISSIPPI RIVER

MISSISSIPPI RIVER

PACIFIC OCEAN

ATLANTIC OCEAN

Gulf of Mexico

In Search of
Two Rivers

One day two men from the Seneca Indian tribe visited La Salle. They told him about two great rivers far away. The men called one river Ohio, which means "beautiful river." They called the other river Mississippi, which means "big water." They said the rivers flowed down to a "Great Sea." La Salle wanted to explore these rivers. He hoped the rivers would turn out to be an all-water route through North America. That would open a trade route from the Atlantic Ocean to the Pacific Ocean.

La Salle tried to get money to help him buy supplies for an expedition. He wanted to explore these two great

After La Salle bought supplies for the trip, he and several men started out in canoes.

rivers. But La Salle had a bad temper, and not many people liked him. No one would give him any money. So, he sold all his land and bought supplies for the trip.

On July 6, 1669, La Salle left Montreal. He had four canoes and twelve men. Two priests and seven men in three canoes also traveled with him. The priests were hoping to teach the Indians they met along the way to be Christians.

The men started traveling south on the St. Lawrence River. They paddled their canoes by day and they camped on the shore at night. Their canoes were light and could be easily carried. The rivers they traveled on had many rapids. Water flowing swiftly over large rocks in a river are called rapids. Rapids can be very dangerous. Whenever there were rapids in the rivers, the explorers would carry their canoes overland.

La Salle and his men reached the western shores of Lake Ontario. They were welcomed by friendly Indians.

They paddled their canoes south on the St. Lawrence River.

They told La Salle about other explorers camped nearby. One of the explorers was Frenchman Adrien Joliet.

Joliet told the priests traveling with La Salle that there were many Indians in need of Christianity. They lived along the Great Lakes north and west of Lake Ontario.

Joliet told the priests traveling with La Salle that the Indians needed lessons in Christianity. Here Joliet is preaching.

La Salle did not want to go in that direction. The rivers he wanted to find were somewhere to the south. La Salle had little patience with others. So the priests left on their own and traveled north. La Salle and his men continued south.

La Salle, his men, and a Shawnee guide named Nika spent the winter near the Great Lakes. In the spring, they reached a great river that flowed westward from the south end of Lake Erie.

They had found the Ohio River. But the river was clogged with fallen trees, and the banks were home to rattlesnakes. The air was full of mosquitoes and biting blackflies. La Salle's men were so unhappy that one night at the end of

La Salle continued on his trip to find the Ohio and Mississippi rivers.

August they all ran away, leaving La Salle and Nika alone.

With Nika's help, La Salle found his way back to Montreal. He had spent all his money, so he went back to trading for furs. In the spring of 1671, they went to Quebec to get the support of the French governor of New France, Louis de Buade, Count of Frontenac. Even with the problems he had earlier, La Salle still wanted to find the great Mississippi River and claim it for France.

La Salle talked to the governor of New France. The governor liked La Salle's ideas and met with Iroquois leaders. France and the Iroquois signed a peace treaty. Shown here is the peace meeting between the French and the Iroquois.

Fort Frontenac

Governor Frontenac liked La Salle's plans. On June 3, 1673, Frontenac left Quebec to meet with Iroquois Indian leaders. Soldiers in fine uniforms went with him. The Iroquois were very impressed. At a meeting on July 13, Frontenac gave the Iroquois leaders many gifts and told them that France had no plans to go to war with them.

The French and the Iroquois signed a peace treaty. They agreed to trade furs. The French would also be allowed to build a fort along the shore of Lake Ontario.

The French soon began building the fort that they called Fort Frontenac.

In 1674, La Salle sailed back to France to talk to the king. He had to wait for an appointment. Finally, in May 1675, La Salle told King Louis about the great rivers and the new lands. He asked the king for permission to trade with the Indians, explore new lands, and to add land to New France. King Louis made La Salle a nobleman and named him governor of Fort Frontenac. He also gave La Salle a lot of land, and granted all his requests. La Salle convinced friends and family to lend him money. Then he returned to New France.

King Louis XVI made La Salle the governor of Fort Frontenac.

As soon as he landed, La Salle went to Fort Frontenac. La Salle set up trading posts. His men built a new fort and houses for the soldiers. By 1676, they had built a mill to grind wheat and corn into flour. They also built a bakery. They cleared the forests so new settlers would be able to start farming as soon as they arrived. La Salle made Fort Frontenac a great success, but once again he had used up all his money.

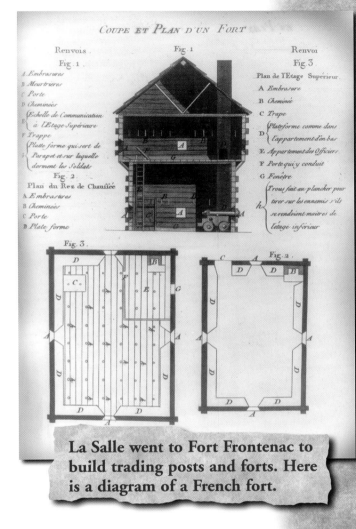

La Salle went to Fort Frontenac to build trading posts and forts. Here is a diagram of a French fort.

The people in Montreal became very unhappy with La Salle because the Indians no longer had to travel 180 miles to that city to trade. Instead, they went to Fort Frontenac to trade furs for goods.

French soldiers, or musketeers, lived
in forts and houses in Fort Frontenac.

In September 1677, La Salle made another trip back to France. He wanted to ask the king for permission to explore the land for France and build more forts for trade with the Indians. He took with him a map showing the Mississippi and Ohio rivers. The map was drawn up from stories told to La Salle by the Indians. It showed where French forts should be built. The soldiers at these forts would keep the lands and the rivers under French rule. King Louis liked the plan and gave La Salle his permission. Once again, La Salle convinced his family and friends to give him money for his latest adventure.

La Salle and his men sailed across Lake
Erie and Lake Huron.

Griffin

In the fall of 1678, La Salle returned to New France. He had picked about thirty skilled workers to return with him. Among them was a soldier named Henri de Tonty. He was a good friend of La Salle.

In the spring and summer of 1679, La Salle and his men built a ship that they named *Griffin*.

On August 7, 1679, La Salle set sail across Lake Erie. *Griffin* carried the men across Lake Erie and Lake Huron. At the point where Lake Huron and Lake Michigan meet, the small settlement of Mackinac had been built. Tonty and some of the men stayed at

Mackinac. They hoped to get more information about the rivers. Tonty tried to get some more men to join La Salle on the next expedition.

La Salle, with the rest of the men, sailed *Griffin* south on Lake Michigan until it reached Green Bay. Here the men traded with the Indians. The goods were loaded on to *Griffin*. La Salle had a plan. Some of the men were to sail the ship back to a settlement called Niagara,

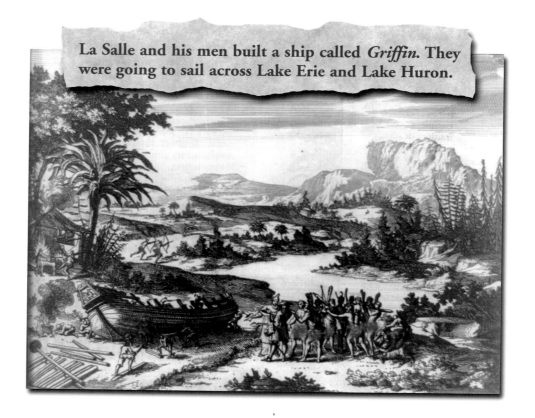

La Salle and his men built a ship called *Griffin*. They were going to sail across Lake Erie and Lake Huron.

which was located at the northeastern tip of Lake Erie. When they reached Niagara they were to sell the goods at the trading post. Then they were to sail the ship back to Mackinac. They were to pick up Tonty and the other men.

While *Griffin* was gone, La Salle and the others would paddle canoes from Green Bay to the southern tip of Lake Michigan. Here they would wait for *Griffin*. Then the search for the Mississippi and the Ohio rivers would begin.

It was a good plan, but it did not work. On November 1, 1679, La Salle reached the southern end of Lake Michigan. There he had planned to meet Tonty and the other men. The rest of

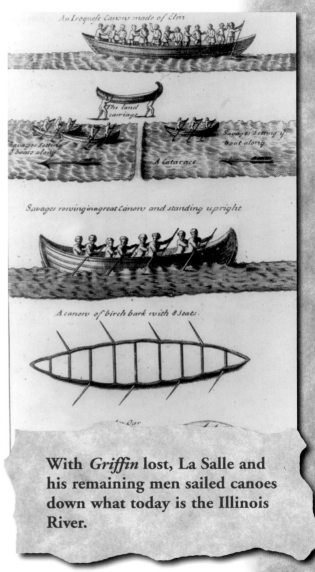

With *Griffin* lost, La Salle and his remaining men sailed canoes down what today is the Illinois River.

the expedition was nowhere in sight. It was getting colder. La Salle and his men built a small fort.

It was November 20, 1679, when Tonty and the rest of the men arrived at the fort. They brought bad news. *Griffin* never arrived at Niagara. The ship was lost somewhere on one of the lakes. It was never seen again.

The explorers went on. Thirty men traveled in eight canoes down the river that today is called the Illinois River. They built a small fort on a hill overlooking the

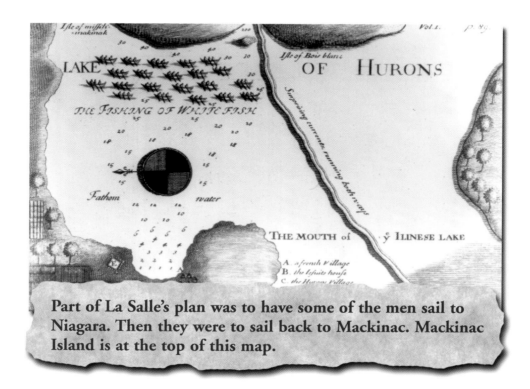

Part of La Salle's plan was to have some of the men sail to Niagara. Then they were to sail back to Mackinac. Mackinac Island is at the top of this map.

river. They named it Fort Crèvecoeur (Heartbreak). La Salle and his men stayed at this fort for the winter.

By March 1680, food was getting very low. La Salle decided that he and five men would go back to Montreal to buy supplies. Tonty and sixteen men would stay at Fort Heartbreak. They would build a ship strong enough to carry the expedition down the rivers. La Salle would return as soon as possible with food and supplies.

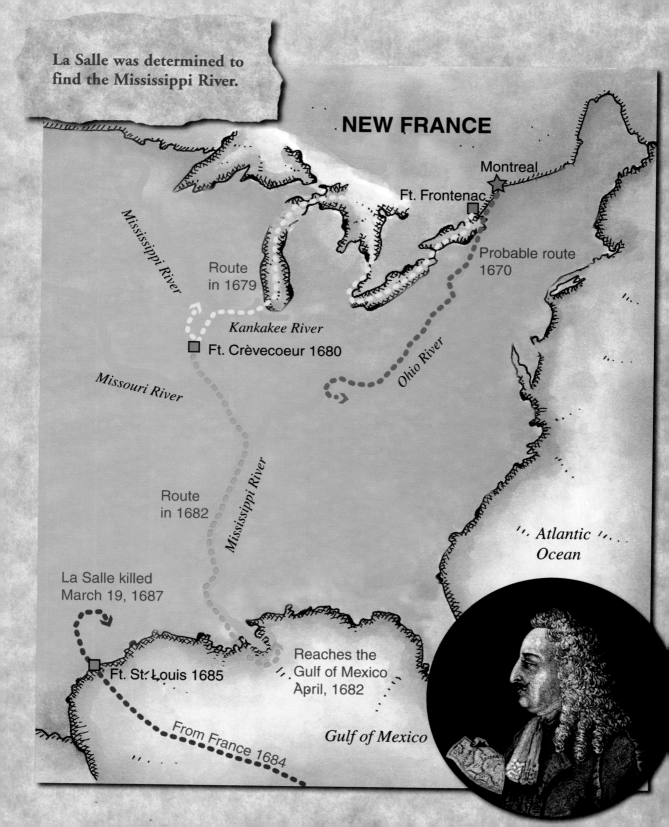

La Salle was determined to find the Mississippi River.

NEW FRANCE

Montreal

Ft. Frontenac

Probable route 1670

Mississippi River

Route in 1679

Kankakee River

☐ Ft. Crèvecoeur 1680

Missouri River

Ohio River

Route in 1682

Mississippi River

La Salle killed March 19, 1687

Atlantic Ocean

Ft. St. Louis 1685

Reaches the Gulf of Mexico April, 1682

From France 1684

Gulf of Mexico

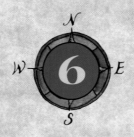

Down the Mississippi

As soon as La Salle arrived in Montreal, he hired twenty-five men to go back with him to Fort Heartbreak. Some of the men were carpenters and others were soldiers. It took La Salle only one week to buy the supplies that he needed. Then he and his men started back to Fort Heartbreak.

On the return trip to Fort Heartbreak, he met two fur trappers. The trappers had bad news. They told La Salle that shortly after he started out for Montreal, most of the men left Fort Heartbreak. Before they left, the men destroyed everything in the fort.

When the men stopped in the evening, they explored the land and hunted buffalo.

La Salle hurried to Fort Heartbreak. There he found the fort completely destroyed, and there was no sign of Tonty. The weather began getting colder. La Salle and his men built winter shelters. They spent the winter of 1680–1681 in these shelters along the shores of Lake Michigan. La Salle met some Indians who told him where Tonty was and that he was safe and well.

La Salle started to look for Tonty in the spring. As soon as he found him, they once again traveled back to Montreal. Here they bought supplies for another try at finding the Mississippi River. They traveled with thirty Frenchmen and about one hundred Indians. La Salle and Tonty did not build another boat to go down the river. This time they used canoes.

On February 13, 1682, La Salle finally reached the Mississippi River. The men traveled down the river during the day. At the end of each day, they brought the canoes ashore. In the evening, the men explored the land as they hunted for turkey, deer, and buffalo.

As La Salle and his men traveled down the river, they made friends at many Indian villages.

As they traveled down the river, the explorers met Indians along the way. La Salle met with the chiefs and made friends with the tribes. At each village, La Salle set up a cross, raised the flag of France, and claimed the land for King Louis XIV.

When La Salle finally reached the mouth of the Mississippi River, he claimed all the land for King Louis.

On April 6, 1682, the explorers reached a point where the river divided into three smaller rivers. This was near where New Orleans is today. La Salle divided the men into three groups. He took some men down the most western river. Tonty and some others went down the middle river. The rest of the men went down the eastern river.

On April 9, 1682, La Salle reached the mouth

of the Mississippi River. He watched as the river flowed into the Gulf of Mexico. Then La Salle made a speech and claimed all the land around the river for King Louis. He named the land Louisiana in honor of the king.

La Salle's long journey had ended. He was the first European to travel all way down the Mississippi River. He had given France claim to a huge area of land in America.

King Louis wanted La Salle to start a settlement at the mouth of the Mississippi River.

Ambushed!

La Salle started to make his way back to New France. He wanted to tell people about his great discovery. But La Salle became very ill. He was too ill to travel. So he sent Tonty to New France to tell of the discovery.

Tonty learned that a new governor, Lefèvre de La Barre, had been chosen to replace Governor Frontenac. The new governor did not like La Salle. He seized La Salle's forts and told the Iroquois to kill La Salle if they found him.

After he got well, La Salle decided to sail back to France in the fall of 1683 to talk to King Louis.

The king wanted La Salle to start a French settlement

La Salle set sail for America to settle the land around the mouth of the Mississippi River. He did not realize that he had landed 400 miles west of it.

at the mouth of the Mississippi River. Then the French would be able to control the ships coming down the river and the lands around it. The king also sent a message to Governor La Barre telling him to give the forts back to La Salle.

On July 24, 1684, La Salle set sail for America. The king had given La Salle four ships. The ships carried about 300 men, women, children, and supplies to start the new settlement.

When La Salle reached the Gulf of Mexico, the ships missed the mouth of the Mississippi River. They sailed about 400 miles too far west. With food and water running out, La Salle went ashore on the land that is today Texas. He decided to build a settlement there. The settlement was called Fort St. Louis.

At the settlement, the people were having trouble.

Many were not happy with La Salle. The seeds the settlers had brought from France did not grow because the weather was too hot. Many of the people died from rattlesnake bites. Some died from eating poisonous plants. They were always worried about attacks from Indians. In 1685, 150 settlers had come ashore. Two years later, only forty settlers were left.

In January 1687, La Salle, his brother Abbé Cavelier, their nephew Crevel de Moranger, and twenty-eight other men headed north to try to find the Mississippi River.

On March 15, the men camped near the Trinity River. La Salle sent men to find food. They killed two buffalo. On the way back to camp, Moranger argued with two men named Dahaut and Liotot. During the night, while Moranger

La Salle sailed 400 miles too far west. The settlers were not happy, but they built a settlement there. They tried to grow food but the weather was too hot.

La Salle was shot and killed by his own men.

was sleeping, the hunters killed him and two others.

When the men did not return, La Salle went to look for them. Dahaut and Liotot were hiding and waiting for him. On March 18, 1687, as La Salle neared the camp, there was a gunshot. La Salle was shot and killed.

The land that La Salle had claimed for France is known as the Louisiana Territory. His explorations of the Mississippi River helped open this land to settlers.

In 1803, Thomas Jefferson was president of the United States. He bought this land from France for $15 million. This became known as the Louisiana Purchase. It doubled the size of the United States. Today, the effect of the French who settled along the Mississippi can still be found in several cities along the river.

Timeline

1643—René-Robert Cavelier, Sieur de La Salle is born in Rouen, France.

1666—Arrives in New France in present-day Canada.

1669—Starts out on his first expedition to find the Mississippi and Ohio rivers.

1671—Returns to Montreal.

1674—Goes back to France to get support from King Louis XIV.

1675—Builds Fort Frontenac; returns to France to get more money.

1679—Builds *Griffin*; later the ship disappears.

1682—Reaches the mouth of the Mississippi River.

1683—Goes to see King Louis to get support from the king again; the ships miss the mouth of the Mississippi River.

1685—Settlers go ashore in the area that today is Texas.

1687—La Salle is killed by his own men.

1803—The Louisiana Territory becomes part of the United States.

Words to Know

carpenter—A person who works with wood and builds and repairs things.

Christianity—A religion based on the teachings of Jesus Christ.

claim—To show ownership of something.

expedition—A journey or voyage taken for a special reason.

explorer—A person who travels in search of new places.

fort—A strong building usually protected by soldiers.

mouth (of a river)—A place where a stream or river enters a larger body of water.

pirate—A person who attacks and robs ships.

settler—A person who goes to live in a new country or region.

settlement—A small village.

territory—A land, an area, or a region.

treaty—An agreement between two or more nations.

Learn More About
La Salle

Books

Donaldson-Forbes, Jeff. *La Salle*. New York: Rosen Publishing Company, 2002.

Faber, Harold. *LaSalle: Down the Mississippi*. Tarrytown, N.Y.: Benchmark Books, 2002.

Goodman, Joan Elizabeth. *Despite All Obstacles: La Salle and the Conquest of the Mississippi*. Ontario, Canada: Firefly Books, 2001.

Kline, Trish. *Robert La Salle*. Vero Beach, Fla.: Rourke Publishing, 2002.

Internet Addresses

The Texas Historical Commission: The La Salle Project
<http://www.thc.state.tx.us/lasalle/lasdefault.html>
Click on the links to find out more about Belle and La Salle.

**René-Robert Cavelier, Sieur de La Salle:
North American Explorer**
<http://www.enchantedlearning.com/explorers/page/l/lasalle.shtml>
Learn more about La Salle from this site from Enchanted Learning.

Index